Hover for a Day

Written by Charles Collins
Illustrated by Jerry Seltzer

ISBN-13: 978-1-60131-004-0

Copyright © 2006
Printed in the United States of America

To order additional copies
Please go to:
www.BigTentBooks.com

115 Bluebill Dr.
Savannah,GA 31419
US United States

This book was published with the assistance of the helpful folks at DragonPencil.

www.DragonPencil.com

This work is dedicated to

Michael and Kevin

…and to those people who amble into your life

and inspire you to complete the race.

It was 7:00 AM and the morning sunlight had just burst through Chris' bedroom window. It steadily crept across the cluttered floor, then over Chris' baseball blanket, until the entire room was drenched in its glare. As Chris rubbed his sleepy squinting eyes he suddenly remembered ... today was the day!

Chris was thirteen and liked by everyone. His unruly blonde hair seemed to compliment his constant grin and playful personality. His best friend and loyal companion was his dog, Harley. Every day when Chris came home from school, Harley, a happy-go-lucky boxer, clumsily chased him around their large backyard. They were inseparable.

Chris' favorite teacher was Professor Ecoloco. Although good-natured and well liked, the professor was considered a little bit unusual by his students. He sported long unkempt white hair that seemed charged with ideas. Professor Eco, as Chris and his friends called him, taught science at Riverdale Middle School. Today the professor was about to keep his promise, a very special promise!

24 HOURS

Chris learned in Professor Eco's science class that the Earth rotated one complete turn in twenty-four hours. It was during that lesson that today's adventure was born. Chris can still see Professor Eco's forehead wrinkled with the importance of his theory: if he and his students could hover above the Earth for a day, the entire planet would pass beneath them in twenty-four hours.

When that theory was suggested, the students were stunned into silence. Chris pondered the significance of what he had just heard. What came next was even more startling. Professor Eco had invented an acrylic box that when 'activated' could hover above the Earth for exactly 24 hours. The professor invited the class to share in the adventure. A fantasy class trip…they would Hover For A Day!

Today was that day and Chris rushed through his morning routine that included a hot shower, a healthy breakfast, and a wrestling match with Harley. A match that usually resulted in a tie. Chris reminded his mother that today was his class trip, and with her help, stuffed his worn backpack with a warm sweater, his lucky baseball hat, and some healthy snacks.

Chris was ready to go! His blonde head impatiently bobbed 'yes' to his mother's usual last minute warnings. He then kissed her cheek, patted Harley on the head, and flew out the door. The school bus was right on time as it squealed to its familiar uneven stop. The three mile ride to school, however, seemed to Chris to take forever.

The yellow bus finally reached the school and slowly approached the student drop-off spot. Just as the folding doors started to crack open, Chris sprang off the bus. The adventure was about to begin! When everyone was assembled and accounted for, Professor Eco led his students around the building to the baseball field located behind the school. When the field came into view, Chris and his classmates let out a gasp. There stood a large clear acrylic box!

Professor Eco ushered Chris and the other students over to the acrylic box. They stood in awe as the professor proudly described his technological achievement. After what seemed like hours of scientific gibberish, the professor guided the students inside. It was as big as their classroom. How the acrylic box worked, no one really knew or really cared, but everyone was ready to go! As the transparent door closed behind them, Chris could hear a humming noise begin. Then, without warning, the box magically started to rise. It ascended a few feet and then it 'hovered'. Professor Eco was beaming!

The journey was about to begin. With an air of confidence, the professor started pushing buttons on a shiny remote control box. The acrylic box ascended steadily. As the box went higher, the view became grander. Chris began to see the outline of the southern coast and the Atlantic Ocean stretching across the east. The roundness of the Earth was now visible and the continent of the United States lay beneath him and his classmates. Chris was lost in amazement!

Seemingly, in an effort to find the exact right words for such a magical event, Professor Eco humbly started to tell them about the Earth and it's vast mysteries, miracles, and resources. Chris was spellbound as he looked down through the floor of the acrylic box at the wonders below. He could immediately make out the boot shape of his home state of Florida. It was at this time that Professor Eco's mood started to change.

"Florida", Professor Eco began, "is the state that boasts the Everglades, Disney World, Daytona Beach, and the Kennedy Space Center. It is also the home of the Florida cougar. Today, there are only 50 mature Florida cougars left! The land where the cougar had once roamed, hunted, and made their dens is rapidly disappearing. People are building more and more homes, highways, and buildings on what was once the cougar's unique habitat. It is very sad!"

Chris was stunned! He asked the professor why no one protected them. The professor explained that not enough people cared about the Florida cougar to make a difference. He then pointed to the north. Chris looked out of the clear acrylic box in that direction. He heard the professor report that in North Carolina there were less than 50 mature red foxes. They are scarce for the same reason, the loss of habitat. They also needed help. Chris immediately knew why the professor's mood had changed. What would the rest of this journey reveal? he wondered.

The Earth began to move east under the hovering clear box. The views afforded the students were beyond description. The land looked like a melting ice cream sundae while the water looked like a frozen blueberry shake. The fluffy white clouds seemed to smile as they drifted by. Chris winked back. "What beauty," he exclaimed. It was then that Professor Eco passionately started the lesson he had planned for this special day. Chris and his fellow classmates were silent as Professor Eco started to write the word 'CONSERVATION' on the wall of the acrylic box with a large red magic marker.

CONSE

"So class, what does the word 'CONSERVATION' mean?" Professor Eco asked knowingly. Chris thought for a second about the word written in red marker. His mind kept recalling what the professor had just told them about the sad plight of the red fox and Florida cougar. Suddenly, the word hit him, "Protection", Chris called out. The professor stroked his chin, "Absolutely right, Chris. It does mean protection...but, it also means even more than that!"

"Conservation is not only protection, but also preservation, restoration, and the management of wildlife against loss, damage, and neglect." Professor Eco was serious now and Chris was 'all ears' as the day's lesson was starting to get into full gear. He guessed that today Professor Eco was going to show the class just how neglectful people have been to the wildlife, their habitat, and their overall conservation. He was right!

Chris' attention was now focused on the revolving Earth below. As the box hovered over Florida, he was riveted to the site of the vast majestic mountains and the beauty below. He marveled at the confidence the fragile Earth seemed to proudly display. As a large puffy cloud approached the hovering box, Chris wondered what the next twenty-four hours would reveal to him and his classmates.

As Chris daydreamed, suddenly, the approaching white cloud surrounded the box. Chris could only see white. He could feel the hovering box start to vibrate. Everyone seemed startled, even Professor Eco! The box then started to wobble, and with a final lurch, hurtled toward Earth.

"Hold on!" Professor Eco shouted as they picked up speed. Chris was silent with fear as the clear box popped out from underneath the huge white cloud.

The Earth loomed below.

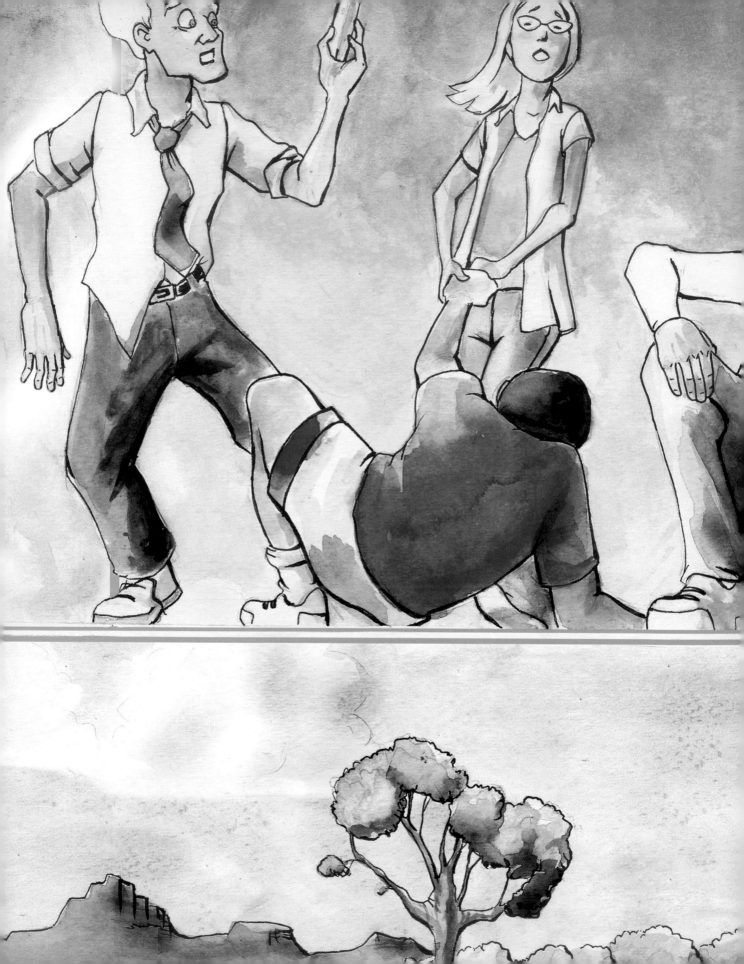

It was precisely at that moment the box stopped shaking and came to a screeching halt. It once again hovered gracefully above the ground. Professor Eco, after a moment of calculation, announced that the moisture in the cloud affected the air density, and therefore, the hovering ability of the box. He seemed back in control as he assured Chris and the other students they were perfectly safe. For the rest of the journey, Professor Eco would guide the box around the clouds.

Professor Eco's booming voice startled Chris back to the lesson at hand. "Look below, that is the great state of Texas. Now look closer. See those small shapes in the fields below? Those little shapes are 'Texas ocelots'! These spotted cats have almost vanished from North America because of hunting and loss of habitat. The clearing of brush country and the construction of highways have limited their range and there are only about 100 Texas ocelots remaining." Chris could feel the sadness creep up inside him.

CONSERVATION

EXTINCT

Both the professor's excitement and his dismay could be heard in his voice as he described the ocelot's population. "Just like the red fox and Florida cougar, Texas ocelots were in such small numbers that they were at risk of extinction." As the professor added the word 'EXTINCT' to the wall with his red marker, he quietly explained that 'extinct' meant: 'no longer living or existing'. Professor Eco called them an 'Endangered Species'! Chris would see many more Endangered Species before this day of adventure would end!

CONSERVATIO

EXTINCT

With a renewed sense of purpose and a grand flourish, Professor Eco added the next words onto the hovering box's clear wall. He stepped aside, his right hand holding the red marker with readiness. The new words, 'ENDANGERED SPECIES', were now up on the wall, too. You could hear a pin drop as Professor Eco continued to write below it, 'a species present in such small numbers that it is at risk of extinction!' Chris knew, sadly, that this meant that those animals could forever be lost to the Earth.

ENDANGERED SPECIES

A SPECIES PRESENT IN SUCH SMALL NUMBERS THAT IT IS AT RISK OF EXTINCTION!

Energized, Professor Eco started pointing everywhere as the revolving Earth slid by beneath them. "Look!" he said zeroing in on the California coast, "The condor can live up to sixty years of age, yet, they are still endangered. Loss of habitat, shootings, pesticide residue, lead poisoning and collisions with power lines, had reduced their population to less than twenty-five by the year 1982

Chris started to think about all the wildlife and how they seemed to depend on one another in some important way. He remembered Professor Eco talking about this delicate balance in nature. It was the science of Ecology, the relationship between organisms and their environments. Chris had to smile to himself as he remembered that Professor Eco's last name was Ecoloco!

As the vast Pacific Ocean stretched out before the hovering box, small dots appeared below. The Hawaiian Islands were coming into focus and the professor began highlighting the plight of the Hawaiian crow. Unfortunately, the familiar sad story continued. It was noted that less than 50 mature birds remained in existence.

The professor lectured on. He told the students that even the largest mammal to have ever lived on the Earth is endangered. He then described the blue whale and how it still swims the Pacific Ocean. The professor also added that the blue whale is rapidly headed toward extinction.

Chris refocused on the lecture as he faintly heard the word 'wombat'. He learned that the wombat population was located in northern Australia and only about 50 mature adults are left! Another animal being deprived of its habitat.

Soon, the students found themselves
hovering over a new large land mass.
The snakelike silhouette below was easy
to recognize. It was the Great Wall Of
China. The mysterious and enchanting
country of China was now passing
beneath them. Chris' excitement was
only temporary. He was about to hear
more bad news from the professor
about a very special animal!

"Due to the decline in their habitat", Professor Eco began, "the giant panda population consists of less than 250 mature adults. They are called carnivores. That means they are flesh-eaters, even though their diet consists mainly of bamboo. Sadly, this is just another animal in dire need of conservation efforts."

As the countries of the Middle East appeared under the hovering box, Chris could excitedly make out the figures of some large animals in India.

"Hey, those are elephants!" Chris exclaimed. The Asian elephant stood ten feet tall and weighed 10,000 pounds. "Even the largest land animals need our protection", Professor Eco sullenly commented! "Yes, the Asian and the African elephant are both endangered!"

Chris kept looking back at India and the elephants. The country gradually faded away from the hovering box. The acrylic box was now hovering above the Middle East.

The professor quickly regained his composure and continued his lesson with determination. "The Anatolian leopard of Turkey, like it's cousins, the Iberian lynx of Spain, the Asiatic cheetah of Iran, and the snow leopard of eastern Asia, are all also critically endangered species."

The acrylic box shook for an instant as a wisp of cloud passed around it. It was just enough to remind Chris of the danger that existed for the hovering acrylic box. Chris scanned ahead looking for another cloud, but the sky looked clear. He felt safe. His mind started to wander. His thoughts turned to the dangers that confront all living things. Dangers that they cannot avoid with a touch of a shiny remote control box.

Chris was almost relieved to see the plains of Africa stretching out ahead of him. The continent of Asia was now gliding slowly away. He was disappointed that so many animal species were declining in numbers. As the Earth continued to revolve beneath him, Chris was very sad and withdrawn. He could only vaguely hear the professor continue to ramble on about the impact on the world's wildlife population from the loss and destruction of their habitat.

As the continent of Africa loomed into view, the news from the professor only got more disheartening. Professor Eco lectured, "In western Africa, the western giant eland, one of the largest antelopes in Africa, is in big trouble. Also, the tiger," he continued, "which can weigh up to 575 pounds, as well as the gorilla, the most powerful primate alive, are now both endangered. Even the large, aggressive, black rhinoceros of Kenya is now in need of assistance. That rhino is currently classified as 'critically' endangered!"

Professor Eco skillfully guided the hovering box away from the danger of some approaching clouds as Africa passed below. Chris' heart was aching for the animals in Africa. As he swung a sad glance at Professor Eco, he could not help but notice a lone tear rolling down the professor's cheek. Eventually, the tear swung free and fell silently to the acrylic floor. There was not a dry eye among any of the students as they gazed silently down on the plains of Africa. Chris knew he had only heard a brief account of all the conservation problems that existed in Africa.

The acrylic box was now hovering above the Atlantic Ocean. The professor quickly regained his composure and continued his lesson with determination. "Right whales grow to be over 60 feet long as adults and are 12 to 18 feet long at birth. The right whale has been the most hunted of all whales. Less than 250 adults can be found swimming in that ocean today." Chris could feel the sadness creep up inside him all over again.

The east coast of the United States and South America did not provide the anticipated relief that Chris had hoped for as the professor went on and on.

"The Atlantic salmon once flourished in that ocean below and now they are an Endangered Species too! Can you see Brazil to our south? The golden lion tamarind of Brazil is one of the most endangered of all mammals! That cute little critter only weighs about one and a half pounds and could have used our help."

"How could this be happening?" Chris asked himself, "and what could he do to help all those animals that need assistance?"

Abruptly, the land below started to take on a familiar appearance. Chris was able to manage a smile of relief as Florida, and eventually, the Riverdale Middle School started to slowly rotate into view below him. The journey was nearing its end. As the hovering box started a slow and graceful descent, Professor Eco called for attention. "There is one more animal I think you should hear about. It's one of the most endangered animals on the planet. It is the whooping crane."

Professor Eco was not about to let the lesson end quite yet. "The whooping crane can be found in Canada and migrates 2700 miles south to Texas every winter. In the 1950's there were only 20 whooping cranes left. Through conservation and habitat protection, their population is now at about 195 birds. When we come together with a purpose, we can do almost anything!" Professor Eco stated confidently.

The professor seemed to grow taller as he spoke passionately and hopefully. "This lesson is not about the potential loss of the hundreds and hundreds of unique species we saw today that are now identified as 'threatened' or 'endangered'. Rather, this lesson is about the power we have to identify a problem and to commit ourselves to solving that problem. Conservation is about finding those solutions and implementing them."

The mental vision of all Chris had seen started swirling inside his head. He could recall the whales, gorillas, cheetahs, pandas, and condors as they swam, swung, raced, lumbered, and flew through his mind's eye. He knew then … he would devote his life to conservation and the protection of wildlife and their habitat. All life is important and all life shares an ecological connection. This ecological connection needs to be protected. By doing so, we not only protect the survival of wildlife, but our own survival as well.

Suddenly, the sky grew dark and the acrylic box started to shudder. Lightning streaked across the sky followed closely by a loud clap of thunder. A fierce storm covered the entire sky blocking out everything. Only the frequent flash of lightning spotlighted the land below.

The storm seemed to come from nowhere! The acrylic box was at its mercy. Chris watched helplessly as strong winds and pouring rain battered the unstable acrylic box. They started to rapidly descend.

Professor Eco frantically worked his fingers over the shiny remote control box. He seemed to try everything. A look of helplessness was spreading across his face. It was apparent that the acrylic box had lost the ability to hover. Professor Eco's long un-kept white hair no longer seemed charged, but rather, out of ideas. The acrylic box was now plunging through the darkness. They were falling out of the sky!

Chris could feel a cold, wet abrasive substance slapping his face. At that moment, his mother's booming voice reached his ears. "Stop dreaming Chris and get up and get ready for school. It is 7:00 AM and it's a beautiful day. You need to rush because today is Professor Ecoloco's special class trip. Also, please tell Harley to stop licking your face!"